Inspirations From
Northern England
Edited by Angela Fairbrace

 Young**Writers**

First published in Great Britain in 2007 by:
Young Writers
Remus House
Coltsfoot Drive
Peterborough
PE2 9JX
Telephone: 01733 890066
Website: www.youngwriters.co.uk

SB ISBN 978-1 84602 916 5

Foreword

Young Writers was established in 1991 and has been passionately devoted to the promotion of reading and writing in children and young adults ever since. The quest continues today. Young Writers remains as committed to the nurturing of poetic and literary talent as ever.

This year's Young Writers competition has proven as vibrant and dynamic as ever and we are delighted to present a showcase of the best poetry from across the UK and in some cases overseas. Each poem has been selected from a wealth of *Little Laureates* entries before ultimately being published in this, our sixteenth primary school poetry series.

Once again, we have been supremely impressed by the overall quality of the entries we have received. The imagination, energy and creativity which has gone into each young writer's entry made choosing the poems a challenging and often difficult but ultimately hugely rewarding task - the general high standard of the work submitted ensured this opportunity to bring their poetry to a larger appreciative audience.

We sincerely hope you are pleased with this final collection and that you will enjoy *Little Laureates Inspirations From Northern England* for many years to come.

Contents

Katie Richardson (6) 1

Abbey Hey Primary School, Gorton
Conor Foulkes (8) 2
Alex Conlen (7) 3
Shay Collins (8) 4
Avehe Kuverua (7) 5
Jack Shepley (7) 6
Shannon O'Neill (8) 7
Cordelia Condron (8) 8
Chelsea Kelly (8) 9
Martin Gilmore (8) 10
Jason Trafford (7) 11
Jordan Taylor (8) 12
Nathan Lawson (7) 13
Sabrice King (8) 14
Sophie Lewis (7) 15
Thomas Laidlaw (8) 16
Thomas Hyde (7) 17
Jonathan Bowker (8) 18
Jessica Kelly (8) 19
Michael Gray (8) 20
Bradley Taylor (7) 21
Bayley Borrow (7) 22
Jake Allen (7) 23
Yusupha Samba (8) 24
Donna Naude (7) 25
Samuel Ratchford (7) 26
Sophie Evans (7) 27
Lewis Faulkner (8) 28
Courtney Hill (8) 29
Megan Jones (8) 30
Brogan Lane (7) 31
Leah Maguire (7) 32
Rebekah Turner (7) 33
Chloe Foster (8) 34
Ethan Bell (7) 35
Matthew Olner (8) 36
Aaron Warmbold (7) 37

Bailey Green Primary School, Killingworth

Name	Page
Georgina Lydon (11)	38
Glenn Herron (11)	39
Shona Briggs (10)	40
Brooke Kirby (10)	41
Lauren Penaluna (10)	42
Elizabeth Wood (10)	43
Bethany Carhart-Harris (11)	44
Aaron Lumsden (10)	45
Leonie Brookes (11)	46
Daniel Young (10)	47
Jessica Gray (10)	48
Lisa Watling (10)	49
Daniel Ward (10)	50
Steven Whitmore (11)	51
Katie Prior (11)	52
Alex Whitmore (11)	53
Ellen Dawson (10)	54
Zoe Knight (11)	55
Joe Green (11)	56
Corey Badminton (11)	57
Philip Welsh (11)	58
Holly Moffat (10)	59
Ashlyn Jackson (11)	60
Holly O'Neil (10)	61
Sian Harrison (10)	62
Chanel Cunny (10)	63
Beth Nichol (11)	64
Chelsea Goodwin (11)	65
Briege Dunbar (11)	66
Victoria Akroyd (11)	67
Theresa Daglish (10)	68

Harrowgate Hill Primary School, Darlington

Name	Page
Katherine Holden (11)	69
Peter Smith (11)	70
Callum Guinan (10)	71
Alex Sayers (10)	72
Sophie McIntosh (11)	73
Zara-Jane Latimer (10)	74
Joe Battye (10)	75

Daniel Wood (11)	76
Adam Thompson (10)	77
Daniel Thompson (11)	78
Sophie Hawman (11)	79
Marc Winthrop (10)	80
Rachel Kilcran (11)	81
Niall Hanratty (11)	82
Joshua Bravey (10)	83
Hollie Gartland (11)	84
Leah Coll (10)	85
Rebecca Carter (10)	86
Emily Thubron (11)	87
Amanprit Kaur (10)	88
Hollie Catt (11)	89
Hannah Bradley (10)	90
Paige Robinson (10)	91
Lauren Hunter (11)	92
Emma Ilderton (10)	93
Sarah Raisbeck (10)	94
Danielle Jameson (11)	95
Sarah Fernandes (11)	96
Charlotte Wade (10)	97
Lewis Davies (10)	98
Sam Read (11)	99

Hutton Rudby Primary School, Hutton Rudby

Scarlett Rose Atkinson (10)	100
Francesca Wardle (10)	101
Hannah Pye (11)	102
Joseph Wyllie (11)	103
Billy Hartford (10)	104
Katie Lomas (11)	105
Jack Crouchley (11)	106
Catherine Harston (10)	107
Kate Laurence (11)	108
Francis Dalton (10)	109
Daniel Walker (11)	110
Harry Jackson (10)	111
Harry Sugden (11)	112
Samuel Boynton (10)	113
Jack Beckwith (10)	114

George Rettig (11)	115
Rachel Greaves (10)	116
Daniel Sanderson (10)	117
Zara Retallick (10)	118
Joseph Pearce (11)	119
Luke Honeyman (10)	120
Sophie Reed (11)	121
Arlen Moore (11)	122
Andrew Turner (10)	123

Northburn First School, Cramlington

Jessica Watson (8)	124
Matthew Hall (7)	125
Bethany Foster (8)	126
Jamie Elliott (8)	127
Laura Strachan (7)	128
Kate Phillips (8)	129
Matty Holmes (8)	130
Will Crerar (8)	131
Andrew Webb (9)	132
Emily Walbank (8)	133
Aditi Kochhar (9)	134
Rachel Baldwin (9)	135
Dale Glenister (9)	136
Tyler Hawley (8)	137
Ellen Turnbull (9)	138
Ben Reed (7)	139
Peter Musgrave (8)	140
Rebecca Douglas (8)	141
Gyan Chadda (7)	142
Reeve Johnson (7)	143
Harry McCabe (8)	144
Matthew Neville (8)	145
Dean Wilson (7)	146
Katrina Sung (8)	147
Jack Redfern (8)	148
Olivia Weston (7)	149
Jacob Gunn (7)	150
Hannah Adair (8)	151

St Catherine's RC Primary School, Didsbury
Becky Cullinane, Roisin Towey (9) & Fiona Taylor (8)   152

St Mary's RC Primary School, Wingate
Georgia Gair (9)   153
Tegan Still (9)   154
Kane Burnip (8)   155
Andrew Nattress (7)   156
Ross Walton (8)   157
Bobby Davies (8)   158
Samantha Davies (9)   159
Olivia Devine (8)   160
Stephen Matthews (8)   161
Matthew Parkin (8)   162
Shelby Younger (8)   163

St Paul's RC Primary School, Billingham
Samantha Wrigley (10)   164
Christopher Allison (9)   165
Joseph Reed (10)   166
Kitty Heslop (10)   167
Oliver Hood (9)   168
Sophia Wilson (10)   169
Ben Sinclair (10)   170
Lucy Tattersdill (9)   171
Calum McNicholas (9)   172
Lewis Robertson (9)   173
Bailey Davison (9)   174
Jonathan Tait (9)   175
Holly Harbron (9)   176
Anna Spencer (10)   177
Elliot Robinson (9)   178
Scott Simpson (9)   179
Alice Cooke (9)   180
Jamie Ginsberg (10)   181

Sacred Heart RC Primary School, Barrow-in-Furness
Joshua Waldron (10)   182
Alex Steeley (10)   183
Sam Moffatt (9)   184

David Jones (9)	185
Alyah Saltiga (8)	186
Ellis Burns (8)	187
Leah Woodhouse (8)	188
Megan Poole (10)	189
Macaulay Murray (11)	190
Ben Speirs (10)	191
Oliver Kerr (10)	192
Thomas Malkin (10)	193
Kieran Hackett (11)	194
Mac McMeekin (10)	195
Levi McMeekin (9)	196

Skerne Park Primary School, Darlington

Liam Walls (10)	197
Catelyn Singh (10)	198
Abby Ward (10)	199
Harry Herraghty (9)	200
Callum Coatsworth (9)	201
George Geldard (9)	202
Demi Hogan (10)	203

Stead Lane First School, Bedlington

Chloe Stephenson (9)	204
Alex Kinghorn (9)	205
Anna Parker (8)	206
Aran Swann (9)	207
Nathan Hall (9)	208

Yarm at Raventhorpe, Darlington

Ellie Stark (8)	209
Joseph Bolton (9)	210
Andrew Clark (9)	211
Matthew Burlinson (9)	212
Imogen Storey (11)	213

The Poems

Here Is The Song I Invented

When I see you calling me I feel so bright
Even when you leave me I feel quite tight.
One morning I heard your voice,
I had to make a choice,
No one else will see
Me and you together
That evening I saw you with another girl
And the next morning it happened again.

Katie Richardson (6)

Fear

Fear is white like a pillow.
Fear reminds me of sheep fur.
Fear feels like scratchy fluff.
Fear smells like a lovely fresh smell.

Conor Foulkes (8)
Abbey Hey Primary School, Gorton

Anger

Anger sounds like angry shouting in my home.
Anger smells like blood spilling on the floor.
Anger is black like a dark night.

Alex Conlen (7)
Abbey Hey Primary School, Gorton

Anger

Anger feels like the trees are falling down.
Anger smells like spiders webs going up my nose.
Anger reminds me of bad times.
Anger is red.
Anger tastes like muddy water.

Shay Collins (8)
Abbey Hey Primary School, Gorton

Love

Love is like a pink rose.
Love reminds me of kissing crazily.
Love looks like kittens.
Love smells like grapes.
Love tastes like hot mints.

Avehe Kuverua (7)
Abbey Hey Primary School, Gorton

Love

Love reminds me of people getting married.
Love looks like Mum's bright clothes.
Love sounds like a song being sung.
Love is white like a wedding dress.
Love tastes like Mum and Dad kissing.

Jack Shepley (7)
Abbey Hey Primary School, Gorton

Love

Love feels like me and my mum spending time together.
Love reminds me of when we go on holiday together.
Love is red like roses.
Love sounds like love and fun.
Love tastes of fish fingers.
Love looks like two people kissing.
Love smells like nice flowers.

Shannon O'Neill (8)
Abbey Hey Primary School, Gorton

Love

Love is pink like Love Hearts.
Love feels like me and my mum and dad.
Love reminds me of the beach and the sand and the sea.
Love tastes like chocolate milk.

Cordelia Condron (8)
Abbey Hey Primary School, Gorton

Love

Love is red like a gorgeous red rose.
Love reminds me of kissing my dog and hugging it.
Love feels like hugging my dad.
Love tastes like sweet juicy strawberry.
Love smells like a bottle of perfume.
Love looks like a pink heart.
Love sounds like a whistling bird.

Chelsea Kelly (8)
Abbey Hey Primary School, Gorton

Sadness

Sadness feels like you have a broken heart.
Sadness tastes like you're going to be sick.
Sadness reminds me that we never saw each other again.
Sadness is grey like a rusty beer can.
Sadness smells like a mud bath.
Sadness sounds like I'm rushing down the stinky fast river.
Sadness looks like a cloud of rain.

Martin Gilmore (8)
Abbey Hey Primary School, Gorton

Hate

Hate smells like red-hot barbecue sauce.
Hate feels like a brick made with clay.
Hate looks like a devil covered in flames.
Hate sounds like Sellotape coming off the roll.
Hate tastes like hot curry.
Hate is black like a sharp blade.

Jason Trafford (7)
Abbey Hey Primary School, Gorton

Happiness

Happiness is like flowers and red roses.
Happiness sounds like lovely butterflies' wings.

Jordan Taylor (8)
Abbey Hey Primary School, Gorton

Anger

Anger is red like a boiling hot fire.
Anger sounds like your teeth rubbing together.
Anger smells like a hot curry.
Anger looks like a mad face.
Anger tastes like a hot fire.

Nathan Lawson (7)
Abbey Hey Primary School, Gorton

Sense Poem

Happiness feels like the sun shining.
Happiness is yellow like the flowers.
Happiness is when you are playing nicely.
Happiness sounds like birds tweeting.
Happiness tastes like chips that are salty and tasty.
Happiness reminds me of nice places.
Happiness looks like fun.
Happiness smells like nice food.

Sabrice King (8)
Abbey Hey Primary School, Gorton

Sense Poem

Happiness is pink like the pretty flowers.
Happiness sounds like a beautiful snow bird.
Happiness feels like my dog licking me.
Happiness tastes like juicy strawberries.
Happiness smells like cherries.

Sophie Lewis (7)
Abbey Hey Primary School, Gorton

Happiness

Happiness reminds me of an angel.
Happiness looks like the rising sun shining on others.
Happiness feels like the wind blowing through my hair.
The colour of happiness is bright yellow, like a daisy.

Thomas Laidlaw (8)
Abbey Hey Primary School, Gorton

Sense Poem

Anger looks like a red-hot fire.
Anger is orange like the orange sun.
Anger sounds like an ogre roaring.
Anger feels like madness.
Anger smells like boiling sprouts.
Anger tastes like cabbage.
Anger reminds me of when people aren't my friend.

Thomas Hyde (7)
Abbey Hey Primary School, Gorton

Sense Poem

Hate sounds like blood falling from the sky.
Hate tastes like bugs inside your tummy.
Hate feels really bad in your head.
Hate smells like a donkey.

Jonathan Bowker (8)
Abbey Hey Primary School, Gorton

Love

Love reminds me of playing with my friends.
Love feels like hearts coming from the sun.
Love is like skating together.
Love smells like roses and cherries.
Love is red like sweet strawberries.
Love tastes like a juicy apple.

Jessica Kelly (8)
Abbey Hey Primary School, Gorton

Sense Poem

Happiness sounds like a ball bouncing.
Happiness tastes like crunchy biscuits.

Michael Gray (8)
Abbey Hey Primary School, Gorton

Anger

Anger feels like steam coming out of your ears.
Anger tastes like sloppy onion in your mouth.
Anger sounds like putting your teeth together.
Anger is red, orange and yellow, like a bonfire.
Anger smells like a glowing, burning fire.
Anger reminds me of getting punched.
Anger looks like fire.

Bradley Taylor (7)
Abbey Hey Primary School, Gorton

Hate

Hate reminds me of the Devil.
Hate tastes like eight-hundred chicken tikka masalas.
Hate looks like Hell.
Hate is red like blood.
Hate sounds like some people fighting.
Hate smells like bacon.
Hate feels like eyeballs.

Bayley Borrow (7)
Abbey Hey Primary School, Gorton

Fear

Fear looks like red fire.
Fear reminds me of my cat dying.
Fear is red.
Fear smells like smelly fire.
Fear sounds like an elephant.
Fear feels like a fire.

Jake Allen (7)
Abbey Hey Primary School, Gorton

Anger

Anger sounds like a lion roaring in your ear
Anger feels like a dark cloud following you
Anger tastes like five hundred chillis in your mouth
Anger smells like rotten cheese
Anger looks like a bomb exploding
Anger is like a devil who's angry
Anger reminds me of Hell.

Yusupha Samba (8)
Abbey Hey Primary School, Gorton

Love Poem

Love, what does it look like?
Love looks like roses
Love reminds me of putting up the Christmas tree
Love tastes like pancakes
Love smells like 100 roses
Love feels nice and soft
Love is red like love hearts
Love sounds like a heart beating.

Donna Naude (7)
Abbey Hey Primary School, Gorton

Hate

Hate smells like hot, hot pepper.
Hate looks like a devil frightening me.
Hate reminds me of me falling down the stairs.
Hate tastes like a bug.
Hate feels like someone's shooting.
Hate sounds like thunder.
Hate is the colour of pink like a pig.

Samuel Ratchford (7)
Abbey Hey Primary School, Gorton

Sadness

Sadness tastes like rain on my tongue.
Sadness reminds me of not having anyone to play with.
Sadness is clear like tears.
Sadness sounds like a bird singing on his own.
Sadness smells like burnt toast.
Sadness looks like my dog that has died.

Sophie Evans (7)
Abbey Hey Primary School, Gorton

Anger

Anger tastes like a red-hot volcano ready to erupt in my mouth.
Anger looks like two bees arguing.
Anger smells like two fish having a fight.
Anger feels like one thousand bees stinging in my stomach.
Anger reminds me of my mum and dad arguing.
Anger sounds like one million people moaning.
Anger is red like lava.

Lewis Faulkner (8)
Abbey Hey Primary School, Gorton

Love

Love feels like a great big cuddle.
Love tastes like a bar of Dairy Milk.
Love reminds me of a red fluffy rose.
Love smells like tangy perfume.
Love is gold like a glow worm.
Love looks like fire burning around me.
Love sounds like birds flying in the air.

Courtney Hill (8)
Abbey Hey Primary School, Gorton

Happiness

Happiness sounds like bluebirds singing in the trees.
Happiness smells like flowers swaying in the breeze.
Happiness feels like when somebody gives you something.
Happiness looks like sausages sizzling in a pan.
Happiness is a light blue sky.
Happiness tastes like chips.

Megan Jones (8)
Abbey Hey Primary School, Gorton

Happiness

Happiness looks like flowers in the wind.
Happiness tastes like pizza.
Happiness feels like butterflies flying around.
Happiness is pink like pink roses growing.
Happiness sounds like bluebirds singing in the tree.
Happiness reminds me of playing in the park.
Happiness smells like blue flowers in the fields.

Brogan Lane (7)
Abbey Hey Primary School, Gorton

Hate

Hate reminds me of madness.
Hate is red like a jumper.
Hate looks like fire.
Hate sounds like booing.
Hate feels like steam.
Hate tastes like red-hot peppers.
Hate smells like hot curry.

Leah Maguire (7)
Abbey Hey Primary School, Gorton

Hate Poem

Hate sounds like a car's horn beeping.
Hate smells like a wet dog.
Hate tastes like apples.
Hate looks like singing.
Hate feels like getting hot.
Hate is pink like flowers.
Hate reminds me of Mondays.

Rebekah Turner (7)
Abbey Hey Primary School, Gorton

Happiness

Happiness reminds me of my birthday.
Happiness sounds like bells jingling.
Happiness smells like a coffee cream.
Happiness is yellow like the sun.
Happiness feels like stars.
Happiness tastes like tuna and sweetcorn.
Happiness looks like flowers.

Chloe Foster (8)
Abbey Hey Primary School, Gorton

Fear

Fear is blue like the sky just before a thunderstorm.
Fear reminds me of thunder banging.
Fear looks like rain hitting the window.
Fear tastes like red-hot chilli in my mouth.
Fear sounds like a scream coming out of me.
Fear feels like a fist punching.
Fear smells like baked beans.

Ethan Bell (7)
Abbey Hey Primary School, Gorton

Hate

Hate looks like rain on a nice summer day.
Hate smells like bacon roasting.
Hate feels like I am getting weak.
Hate reminds me of being hot!
Hate tastes like burnt hot dog.
Hate sounds like my brother annoying me.
Hate is red like burning fire.

Matthew Olner (8)
Abbey Hey Primary School, Gorton

Anger

Anger tastes like a spicy curry.
Anger smells like burning.
Anger looks like fighting.
Anger feels like spikes.
Anger reminds me of being hurt.
Anger sounds like screaming.

Aaron Warmbold (7)
Abbey Hey Primary School, Gorton

Giraffe, Giraffe

Giraffe, giraffe so tall, tall,
Can you hear my call, call?

Giraffe, giraffe so tall, tall,
How do you stroll, stroll?

Giraffe, giraffe so tall, tall,
Can you roll, roll?

Giraffe, giraffe so tall, tall,
Will you fall, fall?

Oh dear giraffe,
Time is so slow.
But you will die,
So tall, tall.

Oh giraffe, giraffe so tall, tall.

Georgina Lydon (11)
Bailey Green Primary School, Killingworth

Purple Friday

Every time on a Friday when I wake
I feel completely useless,
Like a singer without a soul
I pack my bag and go to school.

When I arrive without stopping time
And the school siren deafens my ears,
This is what it's like on a Friday for me
And these are all my fears.

I walk into the classroom
And this is how I feel,
Like a car with no wheel,
Like a rod with no reel.

Even at lunchtime I have the same problem
I cannot slurp the purple with Vimto
Or even swallow my Mentos.

For me this is purple Friday
And is certainly not my day,
For me this is kind of new
And I know I'm the saddest kid in Grade Two.

Glenn Herron (11)
Bailey Green Primary School, Killingworth

Horses

H orses are such fun
O ften out in the sun
R unning and jumping poles
S oon they might have foals
E very morning up and eat
S lowly getting used to the heat.

That's what horses are.

Shona Briggs (10)
Bailey Green Primary School, Killingworth

What Colours Remind Me Of

P ink reminds me of my bedroom
I t's a bright colour, just like my room
N eat and tidy my room is not
K ind and gentle are my teddies

R ed reminds me of my mam
E very time I see this colour
D ragons appear in my mind

B lue reminds me of the sea
L ines of blue in the sea
U nderneath my bed there are teddies
E verywhere just like rocks under the sea.

Brooke Kirby (10)
Bailey Green Primary School, Killingworth

What The Sea Reminds Me Of

The sea reminds me of my nana,
The way she smiled.
I always thought of the sea,
The sea.

The sea reminds me of my bedroom,
Toys all over the floor.
That reminds me of the waves,
The waves.

The sea always reminds me of my big teddy,
The colour is blue!
It's enormous and cold,
Just like the sea!

The sea reminds me of the night,
When the sea sparkles in the moonlight.
When that happens it reminds me of
The moon and stars.

I'm glad the sea reminds me of
All these things
Because I love my nana,
I adore my room,
I love my teddy,
I like the night.

Lauren Penaluna (10)
Bailey Green Primary School, Killingworth

Christmas Day

Christmas day I go out to play in the snow
But you can still hear Santa going, 'Ho, ho, ho!'
Jumping around as I play
Ho, ho, ho! I love Christmas day.
I have a present, big and bold
Sitting in the garage it will be very cold.
I wonder what it could be?
I'm sitting on the sofa
Oh my goodness, it is a Nintendo wii!

Elizabeth Wood (10)
Bailey Green Primary School, Killingworth

My Bedroom

My bedroom is like a reflection of me, blue, pink and purple walls
stand patiently.
My bedroom tells a story, a sparkly lampshade dangles
from the bumpy white ceiling.
My bedroom is a castle.
My tall wooden bed is my bodyguard, it watches over everything
including me.
My room is a toy shop, my sofa is smothered in stuffed toys
And soft heart-shaped cushions.

Bethany Carhart-Harris (11)
Bailey Green Primary School, Killingworth

Football

F ootballers score hat-tricks
O ne goal could win the match
O nly one person can turn it around
T he keeper dives to stop the ball
B all boys stand along the side
A goal in the back of the net
L ong-sleeved goalie tops
L oads of people have turned up.

Aaron Lumsden (10)
Bailey Green Primary School, Killingworth

Pet Shop

N ow I have a new dog
E very morning he eats till he's ready to pop
W ill he ever stop?
F ood is costly for him
O utside he makes a terrible din
U nder the sun he is far too hot
N ow he's too big to fit in his cot
D rool is hanging down his chest
L ooking over his head
A nd his room is white with a bright blue bed
N ext he goes to his drinking bowl
D own the bottom of the garden he gets as black as coal

And . . .

P layful she is flapping her wings
A cting like she rules the home
R ough beak, very sharp
R ound claws scratching hard
O utside is where she mustn't go
T ogether, forever is what we know.

Leonie Brookes (11)
Bailey Green Primary School, Killingworth

Valentine Disco

You can see the boys and girls
Crowding round different sides of the room
No boys are dancing with girls
Because they know what people will assume

Everyone stares at each other
Hoping not to be seen
And if they do get caught
Everyone's bound to be mean

But finally someone tries to be brave
And asks somebody out
He's not afraid of people
Spreading the rumour about

Because of that one person
Everyone's going to dance
With a different gender
They will all scream and prance

We finally come to the end of the night
After everyone's had a great laugh
I have had a really good time
And it certainly wasn't naff!

Daniel Young (10)
Bailey Green Primary School, Killingworth

At The Cinema

Me and my dad walk through the doors
We buy two tickets for me and you.
It's dark and scary, lights are off,
We sit down and the movie starts.

We buy a box of popcorn,
Crunchy and big.
The popcorn sizzles,
I might be sick.

I'm watching the film
With the colours around me.
People munching, *crunch, crunch.*
I'm surprised I can still see.

The film finished, it was good,
Out I come of the pictures.
The doors open, the sun shines in,
I say to my dad, 'That was brilliant!'

I love the pictures, it's great,
I would love to go back again.

Jessica Gray (10)
Bailey Green Primary School, Killingworth

The Waterfall

Shimmering sparkles shine in the sun
As it crashes over the cliff.
The waterfall flows down and down,
Until the rocks don't show anymore.

A log lying on the grass
Disappears out of view.
It goes through the waterfall,
I wonder where it goes to.

At the bottom
It looks like cotton wool.
It swirls round and round
Like a hypnotising whirlpool.

The sunset soon goes down,
The water sparkles even more.
It dazzles like crushed crystals lying in the river.

Lisa Watling (10)
Bailey Green Primary School, Killingworth

Dial Cottage

I see the sight of Dial Cottage,
I am dazzled in amazement.
I see the light on the porch burst into life
And it still stands today.

The door was small
But that of all
Does not spoil the great cottage
And it still stands today.

The sundial shows the time,
The old cement keeps it standing
You wouldn't realise it is really old
And it still stands today
And it still stands today.

Daniel Ward (10)
Bailey Green Primary School, Killingworth

The Lake

The lake gleams as the sun strikes down,
The swans all glide without a frown.
The ducks plunge their heads in the waters below,
The fish swim to the edge to say hello.
As the licensed fishermen go to fish,
They all come home with a big fat dish.
The fish start to die as they get taken away,
There's no fish left by the end of the day.
The leaves on the lake,
They just can't rake
The council comes in to clear the lake.

Steven Whitmore (11)
Bailey Green Primary School, Killingworth

The Lake

The lake reflects the sun's dancing rays
As the messy ducks splash around.
The elegant swans glide past as the clouds suddenly burst
The shower of rain floods the earth.
Creatures hide from the hard-hearted clouds
Showers turn evil and become storm-filled.

As the rain falls, the lake fills,
The clouds take over, the sun fades.
As the lake turns dull, the birds fly to their roost,
The ducks hide, the fish freeze
In the murky waters of the lake.

Katie Prior (11)
Bailey Green Primary School, Killingworth

Dragon

There once was a dragon
How elegantly he flew,
Lying in his lair,
He grew and grew.

There came a day
Many years on,
He was fifty feet tall
And weighed one tonne.

The dragon met
Someone close to his heart,
But there came a threat
And they had to part.

The dragon flew away
And never came back,
This mythical creature
Was about to crack.

So the dragon returned
To his home place,
He felt much better
And had a smile on his face.

The dragon became sick
And started to cry,
He suddenly realised
He was starting to die.

It wasn't long
Before the dragon moved on,
He lay there still
And the dragon was . . . gone.

Alex Whitmore (11)
Bailey Green Primary School, Killingworth

Why Me?

When life is fine you expect everything to stay
But when a part of life disappears, your life turns low
Like a human without any eyes
Your life turns upside down, you feel idiotic
My only question is . . . why me?

Your smile disappears for what seems like an eternity
Like a black hole taking over your heart
It sticks like super glue
It destroys you apart
But why, oh why me?

The stars twinkle but you're still in pain
Not outside but deep inside
I think I'm going insane!
I can't be! But why me?

Ellen Dawson (10)
Bailey Green Primary School, Killingworth

Disappear, Appear

As the sun begins to fall
The glittering moon appears,
As the people close their eyes
The midnight monster appears,
The dustbins crash,
The wind howls,
But the midnight monster stays.

As the night gets darker
The monster creeps around,
The slightest noise of doors shutting
He's out of sight once more,
He comes back, step by step,
Gently touching the floor,
All you can hear is the pitter-patter of his feet below.

As the sun begins to rise
And the sprays of heat come down,
The midnight monster runs away
To hide once more
Behind a dustbin,
Behind a skip,
Take a guess, you might be right!

Zoe Knight (11)
Bailey Green Primary School, Killingworth

The Sea

I went to sea
To see the sea
And what did I see?
I saw the sea.

I went to sea
And I've seen
The reflection of me
In the clear blue sea.

I went to sea
To see the sea
But left the sea
To have my tea.

I went back to sea
After my tea
Nothing to see
So I left the sea.

Joe Green (11)
Bailey Green Primary School, Killingworth

The Sleeping Giant

I watch over the Bay of Naples,
As the silent volcano gently sleeps,
I imagine the terrified families in 79AD.

The volcano awakes,
The trembling din deafens the petrified people of Pompeii,
The volcanic ash blankets the wealthy town.

The vast area of the magnificent Amalfi Coast
Is untouched by the destructive giant,
As the Bay of Naples is blanketed by pumice stone and ash,
Bakers hide their money in the stoves,
Thinking they would come back,
But they were wrong.

At the immense Coliseum,
Romans die with pride,
As the villagers perish in grief,
As they watched their loved ones perish before their eyes.

Corey Badminton (11)
Bailey Green Primary School, Killingworth

At Night

At night the stars shine bright,
(Oh what a beautiful sight)
The moon stands tall
And controls it all.

The owls whistle
And birds sing like a thistle,
The darkness of night
Makes a lovely sight.

The trees blow in the movement
And the wind howls against windows
The lakes stir slowly
And the sea flows calm.

As roads are silent
No movement occurs
As people are asleep
It's a beautiful sight.

As darkness fades
The sun appears
So we will have to wait
Till night reappears.

Philip Welsh (11)
Bailey Green Primary School, Killingworth

Dancing Shadows

As the pink sky fades to black
All the shadows come dancing back.
When the lamp posts flicker on
It's as if the sun had never gone.

People pass in the street
So the dancing shadows meet.
Eight children join their hands
Like they did in forgotten lands,

Floating on a nearby lake,
I see a graceful swimming drake,
Lily pads drift across the magical waters
It makes me as happy as seeing my first grandaughters.

The last thing I see before I sleep
Is a sight that makes me weep.
A single dancing silhouette
Finishes off with a final pirouette.

Holly Moffat (10)
Bailey Green Primary School, Killingworth

Splash

The aqua-blue sea
Glistens under the sun.
The splash of water
Has just begun.

The voice of mermaids
Fills the air,
While the beautiful figure
Combs her long blonde hair.

Her shiny green tail
Sparkles once in a while.
She pops up her head
And gives a great big smile.

Under the sea
Dolphins gather round,
They play all day
And make hardly a sound.

Why her name is Coral
Nobody knows,
Swimming all day
With a tail that glows.

Ashlyn Jackson (11)
Bailey Green Primary School, Killingworth

The Change

Winter wonder
Cold and misty.
Where the snowmen talk away as they melt like ice cubes,
Distance covered by fog and more
The sun is dim like your heart inside.

Ice covering the modest lake,
With sleeping trees hovering like a hawk.
A black error occurs
Litter applied by young youths
Passing on their feelings one to another.

Boats wait for the lake to awake
There are birds flying south above.
Dogs walk by with their icy coats
Clouds give a dark effect.

It changes so quickly
The boats are in the lake sailing like elegant swans
The hovering trees go back to shape.
The sun come back and shines so happy,
It is hot and dusty
Birds flying back brushing by the trees.

Changes, changes, changes.

Holly O'Neil (10)
Bailey Green Primary School, Killingworth

My Strange Hair

Hairstyles, hairstyles, hairstyles,
What can I say?
You colour it and colour it
But it fades away.

Pink, blue, orange,
Orange suits me,
Purple, yellow, black,
Black it shall be.

Ponytails, top knots,
Or in a bun,
French rolls, clipped up,
I really had fun.

Sian Harrison (10)
Bailey Green Primary School, Killingworth

Wild Weather

As the rain spat in my face
It really was a huge disgrace.
The wind dragged me into the woods,
Everyone needed to put up their hoods.

The sun blinded me in the eyes,
How does the weather man tell his lies?
I tried to get to the big front door,
But ended up on the garden floor.

As the clouds formed over my head,
'It really is lovely,' I said.
Suddenly, the sky turned to blue,
The sun joined him too.

The day had faded away,
The sky had turned to grey
Ready for another day.

Chanel Cunny (10)
Bailey Green Primary School, Killingworth

The Spanish Horse Show

The Spanish horses trotted gracefully
While their coats gleamed in the light.
Their hooves moving proudly
For the crowd below.

The crowd clapped in tune
With the music covering the room.
The horses' costumes were perfectly clean
But the riders' costumes are fit for any rulers.

The final finale was nearly here
All of the horses changed their costumes
And their riders were exhausted.
They all trotted out for the finale
And finished the show fabulously.

The sun set into the mountains,
The light began to fade
All of the horses were in their stables
As the night drew near.

Beth Nichol (11)
Bailey Green Primary School, Killingworth

Days In Blackpool

See the donkeys stroll along
As they take people along the sunny beach.
People wait for trams to stop
As people get on and off.

Amusements, now there's a lot.
There's air hockey to play,
Side shows, hook a duck,
A couple of rides to go on.

Pubs to go to,
Places to eat,
Places to play
And days to stay.

Chelsea Goodwin (11)
Bailey Green Primary School, Killingworth

Emotions

The beautiful sun sets so calm waiting for another day
The moon comes up; the sky is black with glittering stars
The moon's reflection swaying so soft, not touched
There are no clouds, just a sparkly sky
The swans are in the sky, they're in a line
They are beautiful; I look up at winkling stars

The trees have two doves, sitting there so peaceful
I lie in the flowerbeds; the petals are like a quilt
I fall into a trance as the ducklings swim
The hummingbirds dancing in the moonlight.

As I lie there, music is playing sweet music
The blackbird adds its special instrument
The tall green grass swaying side to side
In the calm breezy wind.

There is a bang, everything stops
I turn around, one swan dead!
Everything freezes with frost over
Everything dies because morning is here.

Briege Dunbar (11)
Bailey Green Primary School, Killingworth

Pets

Everybody loves to have pets
But there is one thing everybody hates
When you take them to the vets.
People are usually sad at this moment.

They need someone who will care,
Someone who will feed them,
Someone who will always be there,
Someone who will love them.

If you love them then they'll love you,
You will never forget each other.
You will stay together and make a two.
You will always be together.

Victoria Akroyd (11)
Bailey Green Primary School, Killingworth

My Pet

My dog is black and white
When she jumps up she gives me a fright.
When we play fetch she runs like the wind wagging her tail in the air.

My horse is all brown
He acts like a clown flicking his tail in the air.
When we go riding he sends me flying as we jump over the hedge.

My rabbit is grey.
He has a nasty habit of going into my fridge and eating all the cabbage.
When he goes to bed he sleeps with his toy called Fred.

Theresa Daglish (10)
Bailey Green Primary School, Killingworth

Does Mother Nature Need Our Help?

Does Mother Nature need our help?
Yes! The sea is full of pollution.
The ice caps are melting and the sea is rising,
So please help Mother Nature find a solution.

Does Mother Nature need our help?
Yes! The once green grass is going pale,
The foresters are cutting down trees,
While people are using the wood for a sale.

Does Mother Nature need our help?
Yes! The sky is turning grey
Because of the thick choking smoke,
That we're making every day.

Does Mother Nature need our help?
Yes! The temperature's rising high,
The ice caps are melting, help
Or Mother Nature will die!

Katherine Holden (11)
Harrowgate Hill Primary School, Darlington

What Is Going To Happen?

All the gases are killing the earth
And stopping her from giving birth,
I can't believe you cannot see
What is happening to our trees.

All the aeroplanes and the cars
Are turning the earth into Mars,
If only you could recycle a single item
Mother Earth would simply lighten.

All the carbon dioxide and gases
We are letting out in huge masses
If we do want to stay alive
We must stop car fumes to survive.

All the earth will soon be bare
If we do not start to care
So if we don't pull our act together
The earth will be gone forever.

Peter Smith (11)
Harrowgate Hill Primary School, Darlington

Bye!

If you keep breaking climate laws
Soon on the floor there will be no prints or paws.
Sooner or later there will be no ocean
So please, please, please get your head in motion.

In the wild soon we will not see the deer
Now you'd better get your head into gear.
If you keep bringing smoke all the time
You might take a life or two, even mine!

Please don't waste the environment
Or it will be time for retirement.
That time of year will be very gloomy
And for all the animals it will be very roomy.

Callum Guinan (10)
Harrowgate Hill Primary School, Darlington

What Shall We Do?

There's a problem called global warming
To some people it's only dawning.
There's also global dimming
It looks like they're all winning.
We have to be eco-friendly
These two combat things that are very deadly.

All the factories are causing smoke
We can't have because we'll choke.
All the fish are dying in the sea
We're letting global warming take our stuff for free.
It's mostly coming from the city
What shall we do? We can't stop electricity.

If we don't stop pollution
There will be a big destruction.
What shall we do? We need to stop global warming
Still this part to some people it's only dawning.
What shall we do? It's all our fault
We can't stop a single volt!

Alex Sayers (10)
Harrowgate Hill Primary School, Darlington

I Am Mother Nature

I am Mother Nature, listen to me,
The ice is melting; we're drowning in the sea.
There is a lot of pollution in the sky
Don't say nothing's wrong, you're telling a lie.

I am Mother Nature, listen to me,
You're taking the life from every tree.
Look after animals, no matter how small,
We're destroying their habitat and killing them all.

I am Mother Nature, listen to me,
You can't fly away like a bee.
You're doing lots of damage driving your car,
Soon Earth will be as hot as a star.

I am Mother Nature, listen to me,
You're killing the planet, can't you see!
You have made all the mess
So please don't leave me to do the rest.

Sophie McIntosh (11)
Harrowgate Hill Primary School, Darlington

Don't Use Cars

Instead of using the car, take a bike,
To save the poor mammals
Cos using a car's fuel poisons the poor things
So please, please, can you take a bike.
The car's fuel makes bad smoke
Pollutes the Earth, please stop it now!
If you don't, bad things will happen
The smoke makes Mother Nature choke!
Scientists say global warming makes the weather crazy,
So stop using so much energy,
Walk instead of using the bus,
And like I say, let's not be so lazy!

Zara-Jane Latimer (10)
Harrowgate Hill Primary School, Darlington

Save The Earth

I want to know
Why we pollute?
I want to know
Does Mother Nature give a salute?

I want to know
Will animals live?
I want to know
Will they take the care we give?

I want to know
Why, why, why?
I want to know
Why do we make things die?

Joe Battye (10)
Harrowgate Hill Primary School, Darlington

Pollution

Stop melting my ice
It is not very nice
It is getting too hot
And Earth will become like a boiling pot.

And your computers
Are big polluters
With all the electricity
In the big city.

With your cars
Earth will turn into Mars
With their greenhouse gases
They are killing the masses.

Daniel Wood (11)
Harrowgate Hill Primary School, Darlington

The Effects Of Global Warming

We're running our wonderful Earth
Soon there won't be an animal birth
Next it'll be too hot for animals, it's global warming
The heat will be so hot it'll be swarming.

We're ruining our wonderful Earth
It'll be so brilliant to surf
Water levels will rise; we're melting our ice caps
To get the message over, do some greenhouse raps.

We're ruining our wonderful Earth
We're going to love our green, green turf
Our cars are polluting including the DB9
They're ruining our rivers like the Tyne.

We're ruining our wonderful Earth
Soon a hot holiday will be in Scotland's Perth,
Our trees will be bare
Does anyone care?

Adam Thompson (10)
Harrowgate Hill Primary School, Darlington

Save The Earth

Could you save the wonderful plants
And the small and little ants?
Could you save the trees?
Please, I am begging on my knees.

Please can we lose the pollution
And come up with a solution.
The smoke coming out of cars
You could smell it on Mars.

Please try to keep the wood
And we will get less mud.
If we lose all our oxygen, our heart will stop
Our blood vessels will all go *pop!*

If you don't want your arms bare
You will have to take care.
If we all stick together
We will stop it forever.

Daniel Thompson (11)
Harrowgate Hill Primary School, Darlington

Mother Nature

Spring is when the lambs come out
And Mother Nature starts to pout
Because we are spoiling her special Earth
By putting rubbish on her turf.

Summer is when it is really hot
And Mother Nature gets a blood clot
Because she is beggin' on her knees
Please, stop cutting down my trees.

Autumn is when the leaves have gone
And Mother Nature sings her song
Because all the cars are off the road
But now she looks so very old.

Winter is when her friends come out
And Mother Nature likes to shout
Because she has got Earth's control
And now she is really on a roll.

So now I have told you what to do
And we can start helping too,
To get Mother Nature back on track
And then give ourselves a pat on the back!

Sophie Hawman (11)
Harrowgate Hill Primary School, Darlington

What Can We Do?

Please do not waste our environment
Or it will be time for retirement.
People will die because it's too hot,
All the past we will never forget.

This is because of the pollution,
All we need is a solution.
You have set me on a curse
This environment is getting worse.

Please do not scrap our trees,
Or we will have less leaves.
All we need is a winter pine
Then everything will be fine.

Please, please save the ocean
And please help the seas get into motion.
Look at the Earth now,
Can you save us somehow?

Marc Winthrop (10)
Harrowgate Hill Primary School, Darlington

Look At The World

Look at the brown dull trees
Help the Woodland Trust please!
Look at the gigantic polar bears
Their habitat is melting but no one cares.

Look at the temperature in the summer
It's rising; people are getting dumber and dumber.
Look at all God's creatures dying
Don't let that put you off, keep trying!

Look at all the pollution
Please, please find a solution.
So global warming is a killer
Stop it before it gets bigger!

Rachel Kilcran (11)
Harrowgate Hill Primary School, Darlington

Where Did All The Wildlife Go?

If only those humans would stop pollution
And find me a sensible solution.
Now everybody wants to know,
Where did all the wildlife go?

Now there are no more trees
Rustling in the breeze.
Now everybody wants to know,
Where did all the wildlife go?

Now all the trees are burning
And now the hunters are learning
Now everybody wants to know,
Where did all the wildlife go?

There is a huge change in the weather
I wonder if it will last forever.
Now everybody wants to know,
Where did all the wildlife go?

Niall Hanratty (11)
Harrowgate Hill Primary School, Darlington

What's Happening?

Before Earth went Earth's way
Before we came today
We are killing the Earth
And stopping it from birth
If we don't stop the cars
We'll sizzle like hot Mars
If we don't find the solution
We will never stop pollution
We can make Earth better
So it won't go drier or wetter
So while we sit here
We could be making Earth cleaner.

Joshua Bravey (10)
Harrowgate Hill Primary School, Darlington

The Planet Will Die Without Us

The planet will die without us
Mother Nature needs a hand
We all need to help her save us
And protect all our land.

The planet will die without us
So we need to solve the hot air
But then the cold will still come
The world is just not fair.

The planet will die without us
The planet will turn really hot
We've got to solve it somehow
Quick, let's make up a plot.

This planet will die without us
We must help save the world
Mother Nature needs our help
What is going to happen to this world?

Hollie Gartland (11)
Harrowgate Hill Primary School, Darlington

Help Us

Help us save our precious trees
They won't get another chance please
With all the cloudy smoke
Help me please, I'm going to choke.

We need to protect all the plants
And save all the tiny ants,
What about all the flies?

Please help us find a solution
To stop all this horrid pollution
If we all stick together
It will stop forever.

Leah Coll (10)
Harrowgate Hill Primary School, Darlington

Why? Why? Why?

Why do cars have to use so much gas?
Why? Why? Why?
Why don't people recycle glass?
Why? Why? Why?

Why won't people help the seas?
Why? Why? Why?
Why won't people help grow trees?
Why? Why? Why?

Why do people dump all their waste in the ocean?
Why? Why? Why?
Why do people cause a commotion?
Why? Why? Why?

Why do people cause pollution?
Why? Why? Why?
Why don't you make a solution?
Why? Why? Why?

Rebecca Carter (10)
Harrowgate Hill Primary School, Darlington

Why?

Soon you will see no fish in the ocean
So get your head back into motion.
Why?
Don't fish too much in one spot
Move around the ocean a lot.
Why?
All the fish will choke
If we don't do anything about the smoke.
Why?
The world is getting too hot
And the sea will become a boiling pot.
This is just one little cause
In global warming's destructive laws.

Emily Thubron (11)
Harrowgate Hill Primary School, Darlington

What Are We Doing To Our Wonderful World?

What are we doing to our wonderful seas
Could someone tell me please?
Spillages with oil spills,
It is really starting to kill.

What are we doing to our wonderful weather?
Now we have to stick together
Because of the global warming
Our world badly deforming.

What are we doing to our wonderful trees?
Mother Earth is losing her leaves,
Burning them, leaving the smoke,
It is making Mother Earth choke.

Now we have to take action
So you can make a quick reaction,
We will have to save our land
Our world is being tightened by an elastic band.

Amanprit Kaur (10)
Harrowgate Hill Primary School, Darlington

Mother Nature Needs Help!

Why are you doing this to me?
Don't cut down my tree!
You are polluting, so get on your bicycle
Or do your bit and recycle.

Why are you doing this to me?
Don't cut down my tree!
Our ice caps are going away
So help or *you* will pay.

Why are you doing this to me?
Don't cut down my tree!
I am begging on my knees
Please, please, save our trees.

Why are you doing this to me?
So now I have told you what to do
And now I can start helping and so can you.
To get Mother Nature back in the sky
So she could be happy with spirits high.

Hollie Catt (11)
Harrowgate Hill Primary School, Darlington

Why Can't We Help?

We all love our seasons
We have special reasons
We should all work together
In all the different weather.

Animals are dying
Now people are crying,
So few fishes now,
It's continuing but how?

There are so few trees
To rustle in the breeze,
The animals' habitats are gone
When they've been there so long.

We must react now,
Some way, but how?
We must try our best
And never have a rest!

Hannah Bradley (10)
Harrowgate Hill Primary School, Darlington

Where Has Our Planet Gone?

A long time ago Mother Earth's arms were full
As the years have gone by, our chances are dull
Our good friend, the sun, might not be so kind
We have got ourself into a tangle, please unwind.

Please don't take this out of spite
We do have a chance, we might, we might.
If we look after Mother Earth, safe in her arms
Everything will be OK; we will just have to stay calm.

Paige Robinson (10)
Harrowgate Hill Primary School, Darlington

Help! Help! Help!

Our school is eco-friendly,
Help us please.
We are begging on our knees,
Help, help, help!

Our school is eco-friendly,
Help us please.
Don't chop down our trees,
Help, help, help!

Our school is eco-friendly,
Help us please.
Keep the mice eating cheese,
Help, help, help!

Our school is eco-friendly,
Help us please.
Don't forget to save the seas,
Help, help, help!

Lauren Hunter (11)
Harrowgate Hill Primary School, Darlington

What Is Happening To Our Wonderful Earth?

What is happening to our wonderful Earth
Now none of the animals can give birth,
Now all of the trees are falling to their knees?
So please, please, keep their leaves.

What is happening to our wonderful skies
Now none of the birds are passing by?
Because the world is using oils
Our lovely world is getting spoiled.

What is happening to our wonderful animals
And we are losing all of our mammals?
All the animals are losing their habitats
It is not easy for them to adapt.

Now you need to take drastic action,
So you can make a fantastic reaction,
So you should want to keep our Earth
So now all our animals can give birth.

Emma Ilderton (10)
Harrowgate Hill Primary School, Darlington

Eco Poem

We must try to stop this weather
Or it will last forever,
We all must find a solution
For this strange and mad pollution.

In every part of the ocean
There is very little motion,
So global warming is a killer,
Stop before it gets bigger.

Now all the trees are burning
And the hunters are learning
There are no more trees rustling in the breeze.

Sarah Raisbeck (10)
Harrowgate Hill Primary School, Darlington

Mother Earth And Us

Once the Earth went Mother's way
And that's what they always say.
Though we cover Earth with pollution
We will think of a solution.

We would stopping our Earth
And stopping our nature's birth
And those factories with big fumes
Yet they make gases with big booms!

The grass would not be green
But brownest it's ever been
For we are stopping our Earth
And stopping our nature's birth.

The trees would be cut down
Now everyone wears a frown
And if we make this world better
Would you keep it clean forever?

Danielle Jameson (11)
Harrowgate Hill Primary School, Darlington

We Need To Stop Killing The Planet

We need to stop killing the planet
And start helping Mother Earth,
Start caring for all the plants
Or the planet will lose its curve.

We need to stop killing the Earth
Look after all the land
Mother Earth can't do it herself
So let's lend her a hand.

We need to stop killing the planet
Conserve trees to help the air
Stop chopping down the forest
The oxygen we should share.

We need to stop killing the Earth
We've had all our warnings
We have to sort it out or else
Or we won't wake up in the mornings.

Sarah Fernandes (11)
Harrowgate Hill Primary School, Darlington

Save The Environment

Please save all the trees and plants
And also the little spiders and ants,
Please let them stay in the wood
And keep off their homes if you could.

Sooner or later
Trees will turn into paper
If we lose all our oxygen our heart will stop
Then all our blood vessels and veins will pop!

We can't compete with all this pollution
Pretty please, help us find a solution,
All the petrol from the cars
You probably could smell on Mars!

Can't you please help us find
Somebody who will be so kind.
To help keep the environment together
And to use less fuel forever and ever.

Charlotte Wade (10)
Harrowgate Hill Primary School, Darlington

Mother Nature's Words

Instead of killing me in a car
Use your brain and walk far.
Instead of killing me by stripping my leaves
Keep my animals walking please.
Instead of killing me whilst you smoke
Keep your head and don't be a joke.
Instead of endangering my animals
Don't give me the hump like the camels.
Instead of torturing me with an unhealthy job
Grow more of my friendly trees.
Instead of killing me by heating the sun
Have eco-friendly fun.

Lewis Davies (10)
Harrowgate Hill Primary School, Darlington

Our Planet

The temperature is drastically rising
Climate change is happening around
Some scientists say it's rising by 3^0 Celsius
Warming the skies and then the ground.

Gases are all around us
With rising levels of carbon dioxide
Polluting the Earth's lovely land
Lead to flooding on the dockside.

We are cutting down trees which means losing oxygen
We are also killing trees for palm oil
I believe we are destroying trees for no reason.
Ruining the forest and nutritious soil.

Sam Read (11)
Harrowgate Hill Primary School, Darlington

An Autumn Wood

The windswept branches
Sway in the evening air
As the scarlet-breasted robin
Flutters into its nest like a butterfly.

The golden sun cascades
Down behind the trees
While the moon peeps out from
Behind the clouds.

As the animals creep back
Into burrows and dens
You can hear the crunching leaves fall to the ground.

The claws of the trees
Cling to the ground
As the branches tell
The owls to hush.

The leaves burn on the forest floor
Like a warming fire in a cottage.

Sap dribbles out of the trees' lips
As the caterpillar munches into over-baked leaves.
Rushing rivers flow so quietly through the night,
So quiet, so quiet.

Scarlett Rose Atkinson (10)
Hutton Rudby Primary School, Hutton Rudby

My Beach

The shining sun twinkling on the sea, people come
And start getting things ready.
The gentle sea washing the sand away.
Seagulls flying round like an aeroplane in the sky.
The sky slowly starting to change colour every hour.
Crabs waking up in the sandy rock pool.
Footsteps in the golden sand.
Children splashing in the shining waves
Fish playing in the sea.
Mums and dads lying down on the old chairs.
Waves dashing into the cliffs.
Birds being noisy in the sky.
The salty sea glimmering.
People selling cold drinks for money.
Slowly, one by one, people start to pack up their stuff.
The moon pushing the sun away.
The sea starting to change colour from dark blue to grey to black.
The sea and the sand starting to feel sleepy,
The beach is waiting for morning.

Francesca Wardle (10)
Hutton Rudby Primary School, Hutton Rudby

Small Dawn Song

The moonlit river sparkles and ripples, as the moon slowly
gets pulled back by the jealous sun.
Shimmering fish jump in and out of the moon's golden reflections,
Like bouncy balls jumping up to the sun
Before gravity's fingers pull them back to the cold earth.
The last badger cub sneaks back into the dens and calls bye-bye
to his friend the fox.
The squirrel steals the last acorn and clambers back up
the old oak tree.
The sun slowly comes up and fills the sky with inflamed colours,
crimson, yellow and orange.
The morning robin tweets his song as the cockerel bellows out
the harmony.
The old farmer turns on the light and creeps out into the noises
of the croaking frog calling his family.
The sun breaks through the branches, suffocating all darkness.
Morning has arrived and the early hours of a brand new day
has only just begun.

Hannah Pye (11)
Hutton Rudby Primary School, Hutton Rudby

Sunrise

The linen blanket covering the world in darkness
Gradually fades away into the pool of light that is taking over.
Sparkling stars, like diamonds on a bleak cloth,
Fall from the sky deliberately dallying to see all they can
of the beautiful sight.
Beds yawn as people wake up to have early morning showers
before work.
The engine of the milk float roars to life
As the keys are slipped in and the accelerator is stepped on.
Chirping blackbirds get out their hardback hymn books and begin
the early morning chorus.
The sun is finally high in the sky which God has painted with
unimaginable colours.
The sunrays reflect off the clear water and burn the top of the
swaying pond weed.
The early hours have begun, morning is here.

Joseph Wyllie (11)
Hutton Rudby Primary School, Hutton Rudby

An Autumn Wood

The still, darkened wood slowly transform while the sun creeps
into the misty sky.
The ancient trees whistle a morning tune as the wind echoes
off their crimson leaves.
Their lightly toned bark crumbles off their body like a snake shedding
its silky skin.
The welcoming scent of fresh fish attracts the lone kingfisher
for his morning dive.
The curious woodland animals peer round the tallest tree in the wood
As they drag their lightweight legs across the golden duvet of leaves
That cover the acres of tranquil wood.

Billy Hartford (10)
Hutton Rudby Primary School, Hutton Rudby

My Beach

The golden sun starts to appear
The crystal-blue waves walk up and down the ocean
The first van starts to drive down into the grey car park
The donkey spreads out of the old broken trailer
The people tack them up and then wait.

All the cheerful sea creatures start to wake
Seagulls opening their wings and flying into the colourful world
The sun is up and smiles at everyone.

Sailing boats bobbing up and down in the calm water
The happy children jump out of the cars and run into the prickly sea
A new day has begun.

Katie Lomas (11)
Hutton Rudby Primary School, Hutton Rudby

An Autumn Wood

My wood started when I saw a gate in the distance.
I could feel it as I walked to the gate.
As I walked through the gate I could see an autumn wood
in the distance.
There was a colourful waterfall between the tree.
As I walked to the wood, I could see a combine harvester cutting
the wheat near the wood.
When I got to the wood it was peaceful.
There were hills, rocks and rivers.
When I sat under the tree I felt the leaves.
The red ones were soft and the brown ones were crinkly.
I felt the bark on my back, it was very rough and it hurt my back.
It was getting dark, it was time to go.
I went through the gate to the car; Mum was waiting for me at the car.
I got in and drove off.

Jack Crouchley (11)
Hutton Rudby Primary School, Hutton Rudby

My Vision Of The Future

The world is as grey and bleak as a concrete flagstone.
Mist hangs over the cities as if to hide the mess we made.
There are no real wild places anymore.
All the animals are either tame or extinct,
We have shattered their delicate habitats and shot them for fun.
Every ocean is polluted.
Animals drowning in careless fishermen's nets, trapped like prisoners
in a gloomy prison cell.
Oil has been used up and cars are out of transport.
Villages and towns are left leaving no trace of life.
Some people try to get us to go back in time when we travelled by foot
or horseback or carriage
But people have gone too far in time and won't even try.
Trees and plants are wilting and turning into compost.
Hedges are covered in litter for people are lazy and careless.
What have we done to the world?

Catherine Harston (10)
Hutton Rudby Primary School, Hutton Rudby

My Beach

The early morning sun slowly begins to appear in the gloomy night sky,
Like joyful fish darting in and out of the sparkling water.
The first boats appear and gradually make their way in to the
glistening harbour,
Ready to catch the cheeky fish that await them.
The sky starts to change its colour to orange, crimson, pink and yellow.
The pretty sun sets higher and higher in the colourful sky.
The first crabs peep out from the smooth rocks and side-step down
to the reflective sea.
Shops start opening and guests start to arrive.
Children excitedly charge down to the beach, like a stampede
of elephants.
The seagulls cry and shout as the afternoon sun gives them sunburn
and they land.
The first evening star appears and the sunset smiles down
at the sleepy village below it.
The smell of fish and chips drifts over the harbour.
The beach is left alone with its thoughts.
It's the end of a perfect day.

Kate Laurence (11)
Hutton Rudby Primary School, Hutton Rudby

An Autumn Wood

The smell of crispy brown leaves fills the air
Conkers making a little plop as all sorts of different sizes drop off
Fresh conkers peeling off their own shells.
The leaves stand on the ground of the wood
Some are still dancing off the trees and each one knows it is about
to die.
The rippling water calmly flows down to the stream and crashes
into rocks on its way.
The bark on the tree is taken over by the damp weather.
The gentle harmless creatures hop about landing softly on
the crunchy leaves.
The branches droop down on me as I take a last look at this peaceful
everlasting wood.

Francis Dalton (10)
Hutton Rudby Primary School, Hutton Rudby

Kangaroos

Kangaroos are really dumb
Jumping around all day long
All they do is hop and prance
While others just squash some ants.
The Joey lives in a pouch
It's as comfy as a couch
Nothing could ever go wrong
But their feet will start to pong.
They should go and wear some shoes
But that won't be good for kangaroos.
Kangaroos don't live in trees
But they're friendly with bees.
They also love to jump and jump
But they won't while they're got a lump
Why this is we'll never know
Jumping never hurts their toe.
But they don't go to a luxury cruise
They're really dumb old kangaroos.

Daniel Walker (11)
Hutton Rudby Primary School, Hutton Rudby

My Beach

The sun has come up like a baby's head coming out of its cradle.
The waves awake and they start to whisper.
The sun smiles like a little baby.
The beach turns gold as the sun changes colour.
The beach is quiet, nobody in there.
Waves roar with surf thrashing the rocks like a rhino bashing its prey.
An ancient boat sets sail to catch fish.
Seagulls cry making a racket like little girls screaming.
People arrive excited to play on the beach and go in the roaring sea
to surfboard.
The smell of fish and chips as I walk down the glamorous pier.
The ice cream van arrives; people are queuing for the white ice cream
with toppings on.
The sky changes colour from blue to dark black.
The sun goes down like a baby's going to sleep.
The moon goes up, people yawn, exhausted, ready for bed.
The sea goes dark blue and the centre goes white reflecting
off the moon.
The beach goes white and black, the white part is the good ride and
the black ride is the evil ride,
Waiting for the next day.

Harry Jackson (10)
Hutton Rudby Primary School, Hutton Rudby

Personification Sheet

Six and four the happy couple are both living in happiness
With their nettles and have a garden, greenhouse and a beautiful
                                                    garden each.
Eleven is a tall old gentleman from the eighteen-hundreds, smoking
                                                    an endless cigar.
He has a poor family but a very kind and loving one.
You may have seen number thirteen on the house of horrors.
He is on a function and has had four crashes.
He needs a bandage in hospital; he has nothing but bad luck
But now he is brave and will survive an awful life.

Harry Sugden (11)
Hutton Rudby Primary School, Hutton Rudby

My Beach

My beach started as a desolate beach with the soft sand so dry,
so warm.
The cold water starts to heat up by the summer sun.
The shops start to open one by one.
The fish start to wriggle like flags when it's windy.
The rotten fishing bats roll into the harbour one by one.

Families park up their brand new cars one by one.
The fish market sets up one by one.
The fresh fish smell crawls up my nose slowly, slowly.
The donkeys run up and down my beach.
Children play in the warm sea.
Adults lay down on rugs, like sleeping lions.
People start to pack up one by one.
The cool breeze covers the beach.
The noise of the fair is loud.
The beach is gone, gone.

Samuel Boynton (10)
Hutton Rudby Primary School, Hutton Rudby

An Autumn Wood

There was a gate, it was battered and creepy.
I opened the gate, I saw a wood.
There was a lake.
There was someone fishing.
I said to him, 'Have you caught anything?'
He said, 'Yeah! I caught a carp.'
There was a leaf, it was pirouetting.
I said, 'Hello.'
But he moved backwards, maybe he didn't like me and he fell
into the lake.
I sat down next to the tree, it was an oak tree, it was dank.
I picked up a leaf and threw it into the lake,
It travelled through the lake.
I found a stone, I threw it into the water and it skimmed the water.
Then I went back to the gate and thought about all the good things
there were.

Jack Beckwith (10)
Hutton Rudby Primary School, Hutton Rudby

My Beach

The radiant sun shoots up above the red blanket in the morning
Like a Jack-in-the-box spinning out and up.
Crabs crawl gently sideways over the cool rocky rock pool.
The bell of the fair blasts out as the wheel begins to get dizzy.
Fish cry and die as they get cooked for fish and chips.
A song from the ice cream van passes and out over the
                                    desolate horizon.
Arcade games yawn and wake up as the power is switched on.
A workman out for a morning job gets an ice-cold shudder
                                    on his bare feet.
The rocks whisper to each other as the tide goes cascading out again.
The hazy pier wails as teenagers do phenomenal dangerous dives.
A shark scares the people out of the water as their wet feet diminish
                                    in the soft golden sand.
As time goes on the beach becomes desolate and vacant.
The cars yell as children topple on the seat and begin to sleep.
The sun makes one last pattern on the shimmering water
And the spring of the box comes back in and closes for the
                                    night sleep.

George Rettig (11)
Hutton Rudby Primary School, Hutton Rudby

The Midnight Moon

It's time, the moon has yawned after his busy night gleaming
over the Earth protecting us.
Whilst the sparkling stars as if they wear diamonds dissolving
in the midnight sky.
Like being rubbed off a black, dull page.
The sun is stretching over the magical misty moon,
The big ball of raising hot fire has given a silhouette
over the boring tall trees
In the sleepy colourful woods.
People in the small lazy village are waking from their long lost dreams.
Animals are leaving their hibernation worlds.
Morning has come.

Rachel Greaves (10)
Hutton Rudby Primary School, Hutton Rudby

Small Dawn Song

The lorry chugs its way along the solitary road like a lost child without
any friends.
The playful fox sniggers back after a good night's kill.
The farmer searches his field to find a fluffy white lamb has gone.
The gigantic Ford tractor ploughs the freshly cut field as the seagulls
scavenge behind for food.
The fishermen positions himself on the fast-flowing river
As he sees a silhouetted outline of Canadian geese.
The mighty roebuck vaults over the barbed wire fence.
The beautiful, black, shiny horse parades around the paddock.
The blackness of the night falls away behind the horizon
As the burning sun pops up between the trees.
Now day is here.

Daniel Sanderson (10)
Hutton Rudby Primary School, Hutton Rudby

A Tree In Season

Spring
In spring the nature's habitat around me livens up
The birds begin to sing a breathtaking lullaby to soothe me.

Summer
In summer the emerald leaves brighten up the dazzling forest
Whilst the tropical leaves surround me.

Autumn
In autumn the poisonous smell of leaves chase my bird friends away
I start to cry golden tears which fade away on the ground.

Winter
In winter I'm deserted, not a single movement in sight
My gnarled friends have deserted me leaving me tranquilised
and friendless.

Zara Retallick (10)
Hutton Rudby Primary School, Hutton Rudby

Tanka Verses

Happy
I won the Lotto
Now I'm going to be rich
I'll buy a mansion
I'll have a Lamborghini
All for the cost of one pound.

Alone
I live on the streets
No one to play football with
Forever alone
No one will ever like me
It's just me and my teddy.

Anger
I can't get it out
The raging bull inside me
I'm losing control
It was my little sister
She smiled in my room.

Joseph Pearce (11)
Hutton Rudby Primary School, Hutton Rudby

Small Dawn Song

The sun turns on like a volcano erupting
Stars look like snakes' eyes dissolving
The slow tractor hits into action
The golden burning sun comes back to life
Cars open their eyes to take people to work
Foxes, badgers and hedgehogs go back to their dens
Birds start to sing the early morning chorus, as people wake up
The sun starts to wave at the early morning village
The delicate green leaves on the ancient oak unwind to greet
                                                    the morning
The cat flap opens and the cat forces through.
Morning is here.

Luke Honeyman (10)
Hutton Rudby Primary School, Hutton Rudby

The Dawn Song

The stars start to fade away into the corner of light.
The first frosty snowflake slowly drifts down onto the cold, damp earth,
Dissolving into the wet ground leaving pools of water everywhere.
The baby mice start to scamper around the woodland fields
                                                    into their nests.
The sun opens her fiery eyes and peers over to look at the
                                                    sleepy villages.
The headlamps go off one by one as the sun reaches its halfway point.
People take another step onto the layered snow, smoothed out flat.
Finally the sun has reached her point
As the early morning blackbird sings its awakening song,
It's the start of a new day.

Sophie Reed (11)
Hutton Rudby Primary School, Hutton Rudby

Emotions

Happy
I was so happy.
It was a fantastic game.
The crowd went mental.
Aston Villa won the game
Versus Manchester United.

Sad
My grandad has died.
Why does this have to happen?
I feel horrible.
Why me, why, oh why me?
I can't live any longer.

Anger
I hate my brother.
He smashed Mum's favourite vase
That was worth £100
And blamed it on me
Now I've got to sort him out.

Arlen Moore (11)
Hutton Rudby Primary School, Hutton Rudby

Small Dawn Song

The early morning delivery lorries are slowly opening their
wonderful eyes.
Families stroll out to see if the animals are OK.
The milk float finally comes out like an elderly lady slowly grunting
along the road.
The fast-awakening post woman delivers the post like a destroyed
Army fighter.
The brightness of the street lamps go out accelerating as they
go off crying.
Animals come out like they have had forty winks.
God starts to paint the sky a lovely golden colour
As cars go past, the clock ticks, guarding the front room.
The alarm clock goes off, disturbing the friendly family to go
to horrible school and work.
Morning has broken.

Andrew Turner (10)
Hutton Rudby Primary School, Hutton Rudby

The Magic Box

Purple with gold hair
Pink hat
Nose with a circle at the bottom
Stars for the mouth
Swirls for the eyes
My best photo
Lots of strawberry sweets
Thousands of CDs
A pink CD player
Money
Waterfall, blue as a violet
My kind friends
My loving family
A white pony
A fluffy dog named Jasper
Millions of cats that have friendly fleas
Went to Mexico, brought back a cool hat.

Jessica Watson (8)
Northburn First School, Cramlington

Shark

As aggressive as an angry alligator
Cutting through the waves like a blade
Eyes like black crystals
You are sure to be afraid
Hunting through the ocean searching for prey
Watching every motion
Far from the bay
Tail swooping out behind him like a flail
Dorsal fin stands upright like a ship in full sail.

Matthew Hall (7)
Northburn First School, Cramlington

The Magic Box

Shimmering stars
Fire-red rubies
Sparkling white rabbit
Seven grey dolphins in the Atlantic Ocean
A wish that is never to be told
A big fat cat on a tiny little mat
Princess in a coach
Miss Boden in her class
A car comes past
Very fast
A chick just hatched
Northburn School
A very big pool
Moon in the sky
That looks like pie.

Bethany Foster (8)
Northburn First School, Cramlington

The Magic Box

As green as the grass
As blue as the Mediterranean Sea
Extremely smooth
A ruby as red as a danger zone
Solar system
Sky and clouds
Cyclops
Tripod
My box has travelled to the darkest place in Europe
                              where the adder lives.

Jamie Elliott (8)
Northburn First School, Cramlington

The Magic Box

An old dusty box
Hat and stars including hearts
Cheeky monkey
From the zoo
A tiger that will dance
It lives in France
Robin that sings
Sweet and soft
Makes me cry a lot
A plant that talks
Puppies playing drums
Forty-two devils
With pointy little horns
It went to Mexico
It got me a hat
Went to the park
Swinging around
So high touched the sky
As high as a plane
Next Northburn School
With laughs and cheers
Everybody having fun.

Laura Strachan (7)
Northburn First School, Cramlington

The Magic Box

Featured with stars
Jewels so bright
Sequins all shiny
Coloured tinsel covered
Dotted blue and green
Seven spotted puppies
A devil mad and bad
Seventeen dolphins
Two giant blue whales
That swim the seven seas
A sudden electric shock
Loads of feelings
A box
A crystal so shiny
Ice cream that won't melt
A baby leopard in a stripy top.

Kate Phillips (8)
Northburn First School, Cramlington

The Magic Box

Like a ball
Very tall
Fast as lightning
Very frightening
Two dogs
Four frogs
One wink
Two drinks
Alan Shearer
A furry beaver
October and November
March and December
Australia and France
My best pants
Sweet as pie
Small as a fly
Loaf of bread
Anne Boleyn's head.

Matty Holmes (8)
Northburn First School, Cramlington

The Magic Box

A playground where the frames go one hundred feet tall,
The biggest sweet factory you ever saw,
The Amazon jungle and the stings off a pink jellyfish,
A giant carnivorous teddy bear,
A pirate ship,
A bottle of faulty super glue
A bottle of spilt milk
All these things sound stupid
But it's all mega magic for my box is the size of a pin!

Will Crerar (8)
Northburn First School, Cramlington

The Magic Box

As blue as the Pacific Ocean on a summer's evening,
Green spots and an orange bow,
Enough food for the whole globe,
The rib of a cockerel,
A signed rugby ball,
A piece of a cloud as fluffy as a piece of candyfloss,
Elvis Presley, a werewolf,
All the oceans, a few potions,
James Bond and a dirty pond,
A Roman road, a big fat toad,
A boat that floats and a Billy goat.

Andrew Webb (9)
Northburn First School, Cramlington

The Magic Box

Golden box,
Ruby-red eyes,
Violet-blue nose,
Diamond star mouth,
A picture of my rabbit,
Three wishes,
A friendly dragon,
Millions and millions of sweets,
Travelled to Mexico
A hat with dangling string,
A massive white pony,
All the flowers in the world,
A TV,
Millions of cats with fleas,
A white bird.

Emily Walbank (8)
Northburn First School, Cramlington

The Magic Box

Stars gold and silver shining in the day,
Sparkling through the night,
Tiny wind charm tinkling in the breeze,
Hot sun on a sandy beach,
Stars, sun and the moon,
Blue sky bluer than the Pacific Ocean,
Happiness,
Fun,
My best friends,
Photos of my family
A silky sari from India,
An Australian boomerang,
Bagpipes from Scotland,
Forty dancers,
Eight seas,
Fifty coins,
Ninety curtains,
A noodle strand,
A curly poodle
That's what's in my magic box!

Aditi Kochhar (9)
Northburn First School, Cramlington

The Magic Box

Inside my box I have wishing stars
So one day I will put in Mars.
Eighty-two dragons sniffing the box.
I will swim in the Atlantic Ocean
But first I will enjoy the motion.
I saw my box flying
But my friend thought I was lying.
I saw my box in the dark, it was frightening
Then I got struck by lightning.
My box flew west then he brought back a nest
One morning when I woke up, my box was blue
When I got near I found a clue.
I saw Goldilocks in the box
So I asked her, 'Have you seen my fox?'
I found sixty elephants packing my case
And two rabbits facing face to face.
My box lives in a tree
When you see him call it a he.

Rachel Baldwin (9)
Northburn First School, Cramlington

The Magic Box

Beautiful as can be,
Baby-pink background,
Glittering, sparkly swirls,
Lilac polka dots too,
A kangaroo from Peru,
Emeralds as green as grass,
Peach silk from India,
Tallest tree in Africa,
Leonardo da Vinci,
The Mona Lisa,
Black pearl (Jack Sparrow as well!)
Life and my family,
My friends,
A wily fox,
That's what's in my magic box.

Dale Glenister (9)
Northburn First School, Cramlington

The Magic Box

As gold as the sunset,
Inside it a fun pet.
Made of water,
Weighs less than a quarter.
A man with a cough,
A big fat sloth.
The Fantastic Four,
A lady who's poor.
James Bond,
A big blue pond.
One pound,
A Bassett hound.
An invisible man,
A rabbit in a pan.
A big fat toad,
A volcano that will probably explode!
Somebody called Trumpet Trousers,
A cat called Wousers.
A man who's cool,
A duck in a pool.
My red jug,
A very small bug.
A black bull,
A pirate's ship with a hull.
One pear,
A huge bear.

Tyler Hawley (8)
Northburn First School, Cramlington

The Magic Box

My box is silver
It's got a pig called Wilver.
A disco diva,
A furry beaver.
One-thousand pounds,
A big grey hound.
A big nasty beast,
World peace.
The Atlantic Ocean,
Thirty-nine potions.
One drink,
Nine winks.
A big fat toad,
A volcano that will explode.
A puppy dog,
A lot of fog.
A sly fox,
That's what's in my magic box.

Ellen Turnbull (9)
Northburn First School, Cramlington

The Magic Box

Invisible
But you can smell it a mile away,
Walls as rough as sandpaper,
Corners as pointy as a pin.

A sprinkle of snow,
The darkness of space,
A mess of a million,
The blood of the fiercest dragon,
The magic of a wizard's wand,
The fire of a Chinese candle,
A spell never to be seen.

The depths of the universe,
The North Pole in winter,
The house of messiness,
A place never to be named,
The castle of a dead wizard,
Ten thousand locks,
And that's what is in my box.

Ben Reed (7)
Northburn First School, Cramlington

The Magic Box

Flickering lights flashing,
Glistening in the moonlight.
The moonlight shining to the ruby-red box
With eyes of a brown fox.
I'm invisible
And irresistible.
As sneaky as a lizard,
As small as an ant,
You're on a slant.
A big head,
A hamster called Fred,
All the oceans,
Sixty-nine million potions.
Two trees,
Sixty bees.
A sycamore leaf
A naughty thief.

Peter Musgrave (8)
Northburn First School, Cramlington

The Magic Box

Beautiful, sparkly and colourful,
That's the box.
One thousand wishing stars,
Heaven, it's true,
Head of a duck,
Bags of luck.
As tough as old boots,
As old as the hills,
As bright as the sun,
But still as pretty as a picture.
Sunny, funny smiles
And weeping wails.
It once went to Memphis
And came back with Elvis.
It still has room for the Atlantic Ocean
And lots of emotions.

Rebecca Douglas (8)
Northburn First School, Cramlington

The Magic Box

Golden-edged chest,
Rainbow, very coloured,
Feather-light,
A tank from 1729,
Guns from World War II,
Nintendo DS,
The finest games,
Lovely chocolate cake,
The Atlantic Ocean,
Chinese dragon,
Strawberry sweets,
Eighty-four ribs,
Coffin lids,
Seventy-one parties,
Massive TV,
Lives in the loo,
Eats some poo!

Gyan Chadda (7)
Northburn First School, Cramlington

The Magic Box

As red as a ruby
Steel and sharp,
Yellow stars cover it,
Glows in the dark,
Dark blue hinges,
Bumpy patched,
A wrestling ring,
A chick that's hatched,
An angry croc,
A bongo tree,
Two teddy bears
And a bumblebee,
A very cool ice cream,
A swimming pool,
A fireball
And a football player that never sticks to the rules.

Reeve Johnson (7)
Northburn First School, Cramlington

The Magic Box

Glistening, sparkling, shining like a star,
Silk-decorated,
A ruby as red as a sunset,
An emerald like midnight sky,
A diamond like ice,
Made of leather, a fiery feather,
And a Cyclops.
A planet like the Mediterranean Sea on a summer evening.
My box has travelled to Mexico and brought back a sombrero
And went to France and brought back a loaf of bread
                          as sweet as custard.
My box glows like the stars.
The brightest light saber.
It lights up like the stars.
A waterfall like glass
And planets of all kinds.
It has rough and tough surfaces,
Bumps and lumps.
A cloud as white as a sheep
And a Martian as green as grass.

Harry McCabe (8)
Northburn First School, Cramlington

The Magic Box

Rough,
Warm and cold,
As grey as an elephant,
As orange as an orange,
As green as a treetop,
Dinosaur-covered,
A dinosaur head,
A light saber,
A sabre,
A monster,
Travelled to every country and ocean,
A secret camera,
Inflatable,
Invincible.

Matthew Neville (8)
Northburn First School, Cramlington

The Magic Box

The biggest tree in Africa,
A woolly mammoth from three million years ago,
A UFO in space,
Four zebras running fast,
The longest sea monster,
A furry parrot with colourful feathers,
Sharks from the Pacific Ocean,
The biggest grizzly bear,
The sword of the black knight,
Some African wild dogs eating lots of meat,
A saltwater crocodile happy as can be,
A snake and a slug playing with a ball,
The biggest blue whale in the world,
A really nice dog with a really long body,
A dangerous rattlesnake rattling its tail,
Two kangaroos jumping happily.

Dean Wilson (7)
Northburn First School, Cramlington

My Box

Tea from China,
North Carolina,
Swirls as blue as the tropical sea,
Diamonds as red as the sun,
A bat of all the colours of the rainbow,
The head of a troll,
A leaf full of looks,
A book that cooks,
A dog that writes,
A little bit of garlic,
Last but not least,
An arrow of love.

Katrina Sung (8)
Northburn First School, Cramlington

The Magic Box

Very small
Also a ball,
All the seas
And some peas.
Two queens,
Eight beans.
Thunder,
Lightning,
All so frightening.
A guy called Kyle,
The river Nile.
A can of spam
And a bit of ham.

Jack Redfern (8)
Northburn First School, Cramlington

The Magic Box

Orange from China,
A big fat liar,
A really good spire,
A big fat crier.
Very rough,
Incredibly tough,
Football stuff,
A piece of leather,
A fiery feather,
A big wide smile,
A small laundry pile,
A cheese that's mild,
A big fat child,
That is what is inside my box.

Olivia Weston (7)
Northburn First School, Cramlington

The Magic Box

Made of leather, a fiery feather.
Incredibly rough, very tough.
Invincible, invisible.
Square, very bare.
The head of a duck, ten tons of luck.
Thirty-nine ribs, Ryan Giggs.
All the oceans, nine hundred potions.
Two gorillas, the killers.
One light saber, two shiny shavers.
Some fern, something to burn.
A chest, a rest.
A couple of fish, a gold shiny dish.
A yacht's sail, a glass of ale.
A crystal glass, Miss Boden's class.
A ginger cat and a bat on a mat.
Cameron Carpenter and a green pencil sharpener.
Aunty Nancy, a French fancy.
Half the sea, my front door key.
A great white shark, a brown puppy's bark.
An Army tank and a ship that has sank.
A couple of flowers and the Twin Towers.
A palm tree and the joint of a knee.

Jacob Gunn (7)
Northburn First School, Cramlington

The Magic Box

Shiny, silvery, glistening stars,
I will put in my box . . .
A pony, a snowman as white as can be,
A golden Labrador for a dog,
A fluffy cloud,
A boomerang,
A horse's head-collar,
A dog's lead that glistens ruby-red.
My box has been to Australia,
As gold as the sunset.
My magic box is one of my favourite things,
When the dog bites, when the bee stings,
When I'm feeling sad,
I simply remember my favourite box
Then I don't feel so bad.
I will put in my box . . .
My favourite CD,
And my family tree.
My dog's life will go like this,
Throw, throw,
Just let it go,
Hurry up and let it go,
Throw it low!

I'll go with the flow to take me for a walk,
I crawl in hedges just to get the ball
When I hear my owner call
I make a splash with a dash.
I heard you call, I've got the ball.

Hannah Adair (8)
Northburn First School, Cramlington

Alphabet Poem (Food)

B is for burgers that taste so good.
F is for flavoured chocolate ice cream, that reminds me of mud.
J is for jam that I put on my toast.
N is for noodles, so stringy I boast.
R is for roast dinner that I have every Sunday.
T is for the tasty food that we all love.
G is for goodies that I have for a treat.

Becky Cullinane, Roisin Towey (9) & Fiona Taylor (8)
St Catherine's RC Primary School, Didsbury

Birds

In the cold, spooky park
There stood a joyful skipping tree.
And in the joyful skipping tree
There squeaked a tiny, winy bird.
And beside the blinking, winking bird
There was a slippy, boring egg.
There flew thousands of birds.

Georgia Gair (9)
St Mary's RC Primary School, Wingate

School

In a spooky, dark school
There was a really massive teacher.
And under the teacher
There was a tiny crying baby.
And the tiny crying baby was
Holding an egg
And the egg cracked
And there came a fish.

Tegan Still (9)
St Mary's RC Primary School, Wingate

The Dragon

In a big, old castle
There was a large, dusty room.
And in that room
There was an enormous old dragon.
And under the old dragon
There was a tiny red dragon.
The tiny red dragon was as red as fire.
It had teeth as yellow as a sun,
And spikes as sharp as swords.

Kane Burnip (8)
St Mary's RC Primary School, Wingate

Dragon

Once there was a dragon
Sitting in his den,
Killing people in his den.
He was as ugly as an ogre
As strong as a bear.
He was killing people in his den.

Andrew Nattress (7)
St Mary's RC Primary School, Wingate

Dragons

There was a dark, scary wood,
And in that dark, scary wood,
There was an old, creepy tree.
And under that old, creepy tree,
There was a scary dragon.
And under that dragon,
There was an egg.
From that egg
There was a hole.
From that hole there came a dragon.

Ross Walton (8)
St Mary's RC Primary School, Wingate

The Toad In The Pond

In a garden is a toad
And that toad went *hawoo!*
In the full moon, a werewolf howls until morning
Until it disappears in the light.

Bobby Davies (8)
St Mary's RC Primary School, Wingate

The Two Spiders

In a cold, dark wood
There was an enormous leafy tree.
And in that tree
Was a dark, freaky hole.
Two dark, freaky things were found.
They started to bite me,
Furry animals came on my skin.

Samantha Davies (9)
St Mary's RC Primary School, Wingate

Monkey

In the deep, dark jungle
There was a mammy monkey
And from that mammy monkey
Something came.
It's swingy, it's swingy,
It's very strong and hairy,
It's a baby . . .
Monkey!

Olivia Devine (8)
St Mary's RC Primary School, Wingate

Super Dragons

There were some dragons breathing fire to light a fire.
The dragons were smart and clever.
They did not burn each other.
One flew away for food and came back but with an injured wing.
The dragon was yellow with green spikes and an orange tail point.
Then they ate the food, the food was boar, chicken and fish,
A big bunch of fish.

Stephen Matthews (8)
St Mary's RC Primary School, Wingate

Rocket

In a dark, spooky rocket
There was an oily, slippery engine.
And in the scalding little engine
There was a tiny, thin pipe.
And on the tiny, thin pipe
There was an enormous hole
And coming out of the enormous hole
The dragon came!

Matthew Parkin (8)
St Mary's RC Primary School, Wingate

Gingery Man

Once there was a gingery man
Baking in a gingery pan
With cherry eyes and a cherry nose
And that's the way the poem goes.

Shelby Younger (8)
St Mary's RC Primary School, Wingate

Happiness

Happiness sounds like a butterfly flying in the sunshine.
Happiness tastes like some of my favourite things.
Happiness smells like laughing in the wind.
Happiness looks like kids playing on a bouncy castle.
Happiness feels like melting ice cream in your hand.
Happiness reminds me of fun in the sun.

Samantha Wrigley (10)
St Paul's RC Primary School, Billingham

Happiness

Happiness sounds like laughter.
Happiness tastes like a nice piece of love.
Happiness smells like a chocolate cake that everyone loves.
Happiness feels like a nice place to be.
Happiness looks like a smile on your face.
Happiness reminds me of lots of toys.

Christopher Allison (9)
St Paul's RC Primary School, Billingham

Loneliness

Loneliness sounds like nothing but silence.
Loneliness tastes like cold and bitter air.
Loneliness smells like plain air and hot water.
Loneliness looks like a dark room.
Loneliness feels like you are alone.
Loneliness reminds me of nothing.

Joseph Reed (10)
St Paul's RC Primary School, Billingham

Love

Love sounds like slow, dancing music.
Love tastes like strawberries and cream.
Love smells like red roses.
Love looks like a big red heart.
Love feels like a fluffy white cloud.
Love reminds me of a furry red cushion.

Kitty Heslop (10)
St Paul's RC Primary School, Billingham

Silence

Silence sounds like a disappearing echo.
Silence tastes like a bowl full of snow.
Silence smells like a bubble of nothing.
Silence looks like a deserted desert town.
Silence feels like the emptiness of space.
Silence reminds me of a skeleton in the sea.

Oliver Hood (9)
St Paul's RC Primary School, Billingham

Excitement

Excitement sounds like a gigantic explosion on another planet.
Excitement tastes like a bubble jumping around your body
and it can't stop.
Excitement smells like air clinging to you when you are about
to explode.
Excitement looks like a lion jumping all around in the wild.
Excitement feels like you want to float around everywhere, you want
to go to . . .
But most of all it reminds me of my best ever birthday party.

Sophia Wilson (10)
St Paul's RC Primary School, Billingham

Silence

Silence sounds like nothing.
Silence tastes like a cup of air.
Silence smells like thin air.
Silence looks like a person in a dream.
Silence feels like a peaceful paradise.
Silence reminds me of people who have no friends.

Ben Sinclair (10)
St Paul's RC Primary School, Billingham

Love

Love sounds like happy wedding bells.
Love tastes like a chunky caramel heart.
Love smells like pink and red roses in spring.
Love looks like two people on a faraway beach.
Love feels like the juice in a red ripe strawberry.
Love reminds me of a bed in a love heart shape with pink
fluffy cushions.

Lucy Tattersdill (9)
St Paul's RC Primary School, Billingham

Fear

Fear sounds like the horror of a ghost.
Fear tastes like a sip of boiling hot lava.
Fear smells like a burning black fire.
Fear looks like an atomic grey gorilla.
Fear feels like a giant hand hitting me in the stomach.
Fear reminds me of looking into a fierce lion's jaw.

Calum McNicholas (9)
St Paul's RC Primary School, Billingham

Laughter

Laughter sounds like a mouse rapping.
Laughter tastes like an open door on a windy day.
Laughter smells like a crowd eating sweets.
Laughter looks like an ecstatic chimpanzee.
Laughter feels like monkeys swinging on trees.
Laughter reminds me of a dolphin jumping.

Lewis Robertson (9)
St Paul's RC Primary School, Billingham

Jealousy

Jealousy sounds like a clown laughing.
Jealousy tastes like plain twigs.
Jealousy smells like a burning fire.
Jealousy looks like the betrayal of a friend.
Jealousy feels like sticky glue.
Jealousy reminds me of my rich friend.

Bailey Davison (9)
St Paul's RC Primary School, Billingham

Fear

Fear sounds like an ominous sound in the woods.
Fear looks like a corpse of a wolf in a coffin.
Fear feels like a head with a brain so dense.
Fear tastes like a bowl of food rotting away.
Fear smells like a sulphur bomb exploding.
Fear reminds me of a friend dying.

Jonathan Tait (9)
St Paul's RC Primary School, Billingham

Jealousy

Jealousy is a feeling no one could describe.
Jealousy is a smell of loneliness deep down inside.
Jealousy is a taste of something you want to shout out so loud
the universe would hear.
There'd be nothing inside, no other feeling digging deep inside
But most of all it reminds me of darkness with silence inside.

Holly Harbron (9)
St Paul's RC Primary School, Billingham

Friendship

Friendship sounds like laughter.
Friendship tastes like sweets melting in your mouth.
Friendship smells like juicy red strawberries.
Friendship looks like smiles on children's faces.
Friendship feels like melted chocolate in your mouth.
Friendship reminds me of happy thoughts.

Anna Spencer (10)
St Paul's RC Primary School, Billingham

Fun

Fun sounds like the laugh of a child.
Fun tastes like a bar of chocolate melting in the sun.
Fun smells like a strawberry sweet.
Fun looks like a city made of gold.
Fun feels like a snowball.
Fun reminds me of a lady who gave me sweets.

Elliot Robinson (9)
St Paul's RC Primary School, Billingham

Silence

Silence sounds like nothing.
Silence tastes like rotten egg.
Silence feels like all the people have died.
Silence looks like a fuzzy picture.
Silence smells like air.
Silence reminds me of before the world was born.

Scott Simpson (9)
St Paul's RC Primary School, Billingham

Loneliness

Loneliness sounds like a little bird humming.
Loneliness tastes like a lonely dog crying.
Loneliness smells like a crooked egg.
Loneliness looks like a heart breaking.
Loneliness feels like a leaf floating.
Loneliness reminds me of bad feelings.

Alice Cooke (9)
St Paul's RC Primary School, Billingham

Craziness

Craziness sounds like shouting with glee.
Craziness tastes of excitement and fun.
Craziness smells like running and jumping.
Craziness looks like a face with a smile so big.
Craziness feels like skipping, it reminds me of smiles.

Jamie Ginsberg (10)
St Paul's RC Primary School, Billingham

Me In A Rage

I have a very big rage, I explode with anger.
I kick the bed when I have a rage.
I smash things up and throw things out of the window.
I charge around and slam the door, punch the pillow
And go as red as the middle of the Earth.

Joshua Waldron (10)
Sacred Heart RC Primary School, Barrow-in-Furness

Me In A Rage

Me in a rage, stuck in a cage,
Walking around all night long,
Kicking my toys and making a noise,
But no.
I see in my head a twinkle like the River Nile,
I hope that's me I can see sitting
On the banks of the Nile
Eating my snack, ignoring my rage.

Alex Steeley (10)
Sacred Heart RC Primary School, Barrow-in-Furness

Me In A Rage

Trembling, grumbling, rumbling and bubbling.
I am red, hot and angry.
Crack, slam and *snap!*
I've blown my top.
That's me in a rage.

Sam Moffatt (9)
Sacred Heart RC Primary School, Barrow-in-Furness

Me In A Rage

Me in a rage shouting like a tiger,
It feels like I'm falling out of the window,
No control.
I scream like a girl and growl like a bear.
That is me in a rage.

David Jones (9)
Sacred Heart RC Primary School, Barrow-in-Furness

Joyfulness

Joyfulness is yellow.
It smells like yellow butter.
It tastes like candyfloss bouncy with joy.
It sounds like angels singing to the clouds.
Joy feels like everyone smiling around you.

Alyah Saltiga (8)
Sacred Heart RC Primary School, Barrow-in-Furness

Anger

Anger is green.
It feels like an earthquake.
It tastes like a hard burger.
It sounds like stones falling to the Earth.
Anger is destruction.

Ellis Burns (8)
Sacred Heart RC Primary School, Barrow-in-Furness

Happiness

Happiness is the colour pink.
Happiness looks playful.
Happiness sounds like children playing.
Happiness smells like a bush of roses
And it tastes like a strawberry sweet.

Leah Woodhouse (8)
Sacred Heart RC Primary School, Barrow-in-Furness

All Day Long

Beautiful sparkling raindrop falling.
Beautiful rainbow in the blue sky.
Rising sun shining all the day long.

Megan Poole (10)
Sacred Heart RC Primary School, Barrow-in-Furness

Tiger

A cat big and strong.
A furry sheep.
Beautiful.
A scary movie, loud and horrible.
A pouncing hunter.
A hungry human-eater.
A smart feline thinking, *I'll eat that!*

Macaulay Murray (11)
Sacred Heart RC Primary School, Barrow-in-Furness

Colours

Green is soggy snot.
Green is slimy goo.
Green is a flying flu.
Green is go!

Yellow is the burning sun.
Yellow is as bright as a sunflower.
Yellow is a flaming house.
Yellow is a golden flower.
Yellow means amber.

Red is flaming fire.
Red is burning flames.
Red is angry flames.
Red is running blood.
Red is stop!

Ben Speirs (10)
Sacred Heart RC Primary School, Barrow-in-Furness

Aston Martin

Racing through the quiet streets,
Shining paint gleaming in the headlights
And roaring engine racing through quiet streets.

Oliver Kerr (10)
Sacred Heart RC Primary School, Barrow-in-Furness

Green

Green is snot.
Green is slime.
Green is goo.
Green is grime.

Thomas Malkin (10)
Sacred Heart RC Primary School, Barrow-in-Furness

Jimmy Blue

Running fast Jimmy Blue,
Crying Jimmy, drinking and eating
Spicy red ketchup.

Kieran Hackett (11)
Sacred Heart RC Primary School, Barrow-in-Furness

Seagull

Swiftly through the air it flies
Stealing Cornish pasties whenever it decides.
Eyes as sharp as tigers, focused on the meal,
From its dustbin home it thinks of when to strike again.

Mac McMeekin (10)
Sacred Heart RC Primary School, Barrow-in-Furness

Me In A Rage

When I'm in a rage I try to knock people out.
Snapping my pencil I scream and shout.
I storm off and I slam the door.
I roar like a tiger trapped in its cage,
That's what I do when I'm in a rage.

Levi McMeekin (9)
Sacred Heart RC Primary School, Barrow-in-Furness

Ice Cream

Ice cream, ice cream is nice and creamy
It is as white as snow
The cone is as crunchy as an old leaf and it is as yummy as pizza
Also as well as this, the Flake is nice and chocolatey
And it is the nicest thing you can get off the ice cream van.

Liam Walls (10)
Skerne Park Primary School, Darlington

My Animal

Saddle wearer
Fast runner
Fence jumper
Stable occupier
Bit chewer
Slow trotter
Apple eater
Sugar lump lover.

Catelyn Singh (10)
Skerne Park Primary School, Darlington

Dogs

Dogs are nice and playful
They like to jump around
And when they finish
They just like to lie down.

Abby Ward (10)
Skerne Park Primary School, Darlington

My Kennings

Shark teaser
Plankton eater
Hook lander
Sea swimmer
Cold huddler
Short waiter
Fast swimmer
Bait taker
Pleasant taker
What am I?

Harry Herraghty (9)
Skerne Park Primary School, Darlington

My Rabbit - Kennings

Fast runner
Lettuce eater
Wood nibbler
Carrot chewer
Nose twitcher
Foot licker
Hutch dweller
Heart sweller
Smooth hopper
Who am I?

Callum Coatsworth (9)
Skerne Park Primary School, Darlington

What Am I?

Word inventor
Space creator
Letter destroyer
Game player
Message maker
Capital designer
What am I?

George Geldard (9)
Skerne Park Primary School, Darlington

Liverpool FC

Match winning
Always grinning
Cup lifting
Great dribbling
Kop pleasing
Impressive tackling
Goal scoring
What am I?

Demi Hogan (10)
Skerne Park Primary School, Darlington

My Dog

Bone catcher
Cat chaser
Fast runner
Messy cruncher
Ball hunter
Good swimmer
Sloppy drinker
Noisy barker
Grass eater
Long walker.

Chloe Stephenson (9)
Stead Lane First School, Bedlington

Summer

S ummer is cool because you go on holiday
U p in the sky there is a sun every summer
M ornings are hot in this season
M en playing beach ball on the beach
E arly summer you go to the park
R eading books at night.

Alex Kinghorn (9)
Stead Lane First School, Bedlington

Emotions

Happy is mellow like music from a cello
Love is nice, it doesn't have a price
Hate gets you in a horrible mood
Laughter is great when you share it with a friend
You shriek so much you never want it to end
Jealousy is blue, your friendship down the loo
Anger is horrible, it is very credible
Bravery is strong but it's not wrong
Crazy is mad, it's really bad
Greed is ratty; it'll turn you into a fatty.

Anna Parker (8)
Stead Lane First School, Bedlington

The Spy

You spy with your eye as you look around the mansion
Gadgets are secret; we are as quiet as a mouse
Secret hideouts are the best places
We steal jewels that are scattered around the house
We eat the food off the bench.

Aran Swann (9)
Stead Lane First School, Bedlington

My Tortoise

I put him down in the fresh green grass
He walks around and he's never to be found
Tortoises like fruit and vegetables
He likes to climb on a muddy mound
He munches with his tiny sharp teeth
He even eats our plastic wreath
Tortoise hibernate for the winter
I don't know if he likes juicy beef.

Nathan Hall (9)
Stead Lane First School, Bedlington

Rainbow

Looking at the rainbow in the view
Red, yellow, pink, green, purple and indigo
Lots more colours as well
As you're getting closer it gets further away
It's like 'tig' and you're trying to catch the rainbow
As you go faster and faster, the rainbow goes faster and faster
I wonder if there really is a pot of gold at the end
It is magical.

Ellie Stark (8)
Yarm at Raventhorpe, Darlington

Rain

I hate rain,
I'll tell you why.
It's damp and cold.
When I play football, the pitch is always waterlogged,
My boots always stick,
And the ball is covered with mud.
I hate rain.

Joseph Bolton (9)
Yarm at Raventhorpe, Darlington

Bad Weather

Sleet, snow
Rain, oh no
Lightning fast
Rain so vast
Trees blowing
Stock up on supplies
Light the fire
Prepare the candles
Light them now
Before they cut
The outside
World, gone from us,
Tomorrow, we'll be safe at last.

Andrew Clark (9)
Yarm at Raventhorpe, Darlington

Wind

I like wind.
When I get blown about
I like running behind the wind,
Especially if I have a kite.
But wind is also bad.
Lorries blowing upside down,
Trees crashing to the ground.
The wind can pull the roof off a house
And snatch the cars off the road.

Matthew Burlinson (9)
Yarm at Raventhorpe, Darlington

Animals

Animals are big, animals are small,
Animals are colourful, but I like them all.
Some can run fast, some can run slow,
Some hang upside down as you may know!

Imogen Storey (11)
Yarm at Raventhorpe, Darlington

Young Writers Information

We hope you have enjoyed reading this book - and that you will continue to enjoy it in the coming years.

If you like reading and writing poetry drop us a line, or give us a call, and we'll send you a free information pack.

Alternatively if you would like to order further copies of this book or any of our other titles, then please give us a call or log onto our website at www.youngwriters.co.uk

**Young Writers Information
Remus House
Coltsfoot Drive
Peterborough
PE2 9JX**

(01733) 890066